EASY PIANO

CALMING PIANO SOLOS

T0105921

ISBN 978-1-70514-728-3

HAL•LEONARD®

Visit Hal Leonard Online at
www.halleonard.com

World headquarters, contact:
Hal Leonard
7777 West Bluemound Road
Milwaukee, WI 53213
Email: info@halleonard.com

In Europe, contact:
Hal Leonard Europe Limited
1 Red Place
London, W1K 6PL
Email: info@halleonardeurope.com

In Australia, contact:
Hal Leonard Australia Pty. Ltd.
4 Lentara Court
Cheltenham, Victoria, 3192 Australia
Email: info@halleonard.com.au

CONTENTS

4   The Approaching Night

8   A Beautiful Distraction

20   Bluebird

15   Butterfly Waltz

26   Early Morning Range

30   Fly

34   Love

38   Love's Return

42   A Moment Lost

52   Nocturne in A Minor

60   One Summer's Day

47   Porz Goret

64   Romances

74   Sea Change

69   September Song

80   Una Mattina

85   When Morning Comes

90   Winged Melancholy

93   Written on the Sky

THE APPROACHING NIGHT

Composed by
PHILIP WESLEY

A BEAUTIFUL DISTRACTION

Composed by
MICHELE McLAUGHLIN

Calm, freely

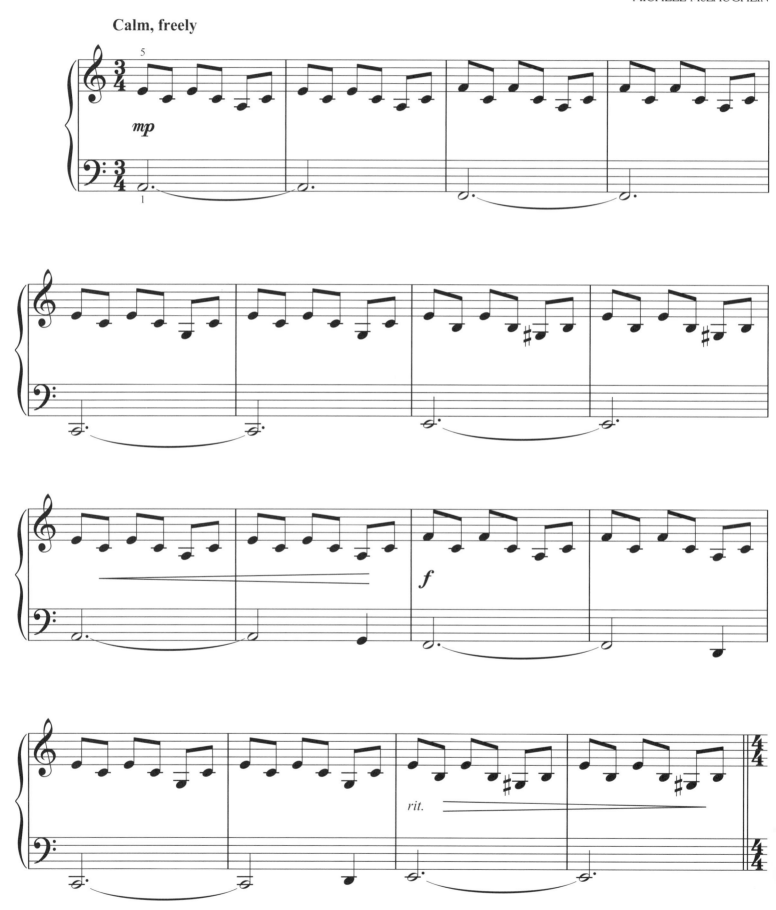

Slower

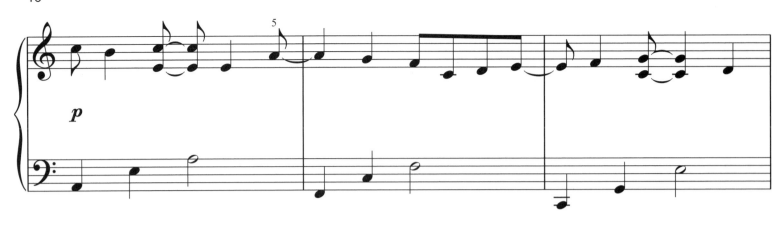

Slightly faster

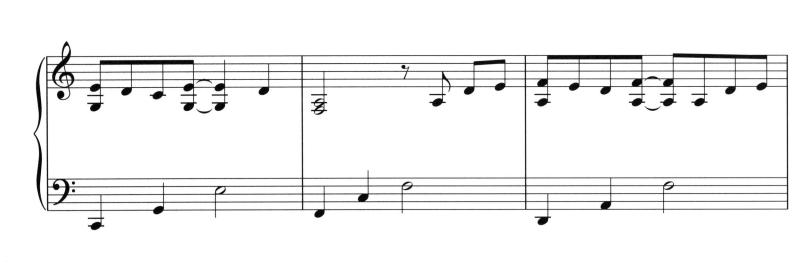

Tempo I

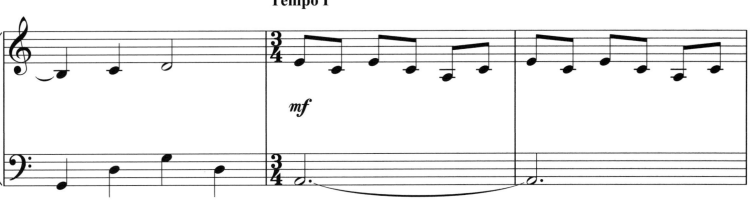

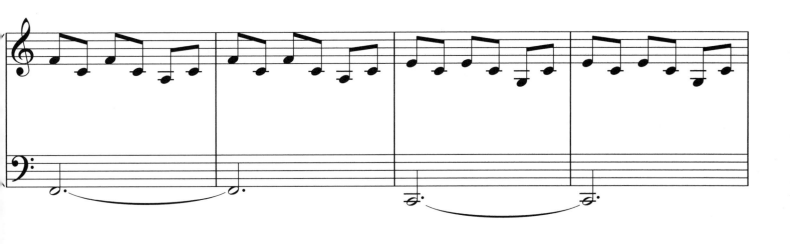

Quickly

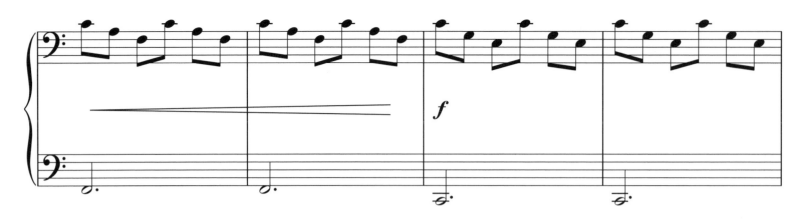

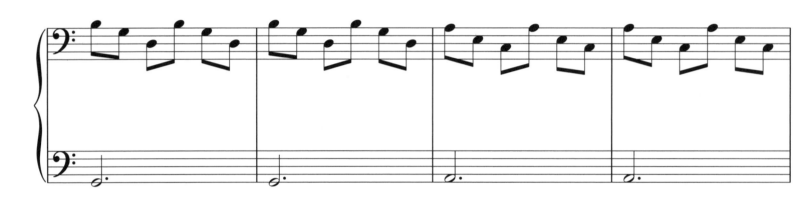

BUTTERFLY WALTZ

Written by
BRIAN CRAIN

Moving along

Both hands 8va

BLUEBIRD

By ALEXIS FFRENCH

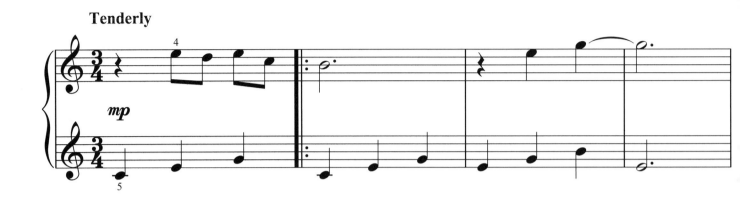

21

23

D.S. al Coda

CODA

EARLY MORNING RANGE

from the solo piano album SUMMER

By GEORGE WINSTON

Full solo transcription can be found in the Hal Leonard publication **George Winston - Piano Sheet Music Collection** (HL 00295534)

FLY

Music by
FLORIAN CHRISTL

Moderately

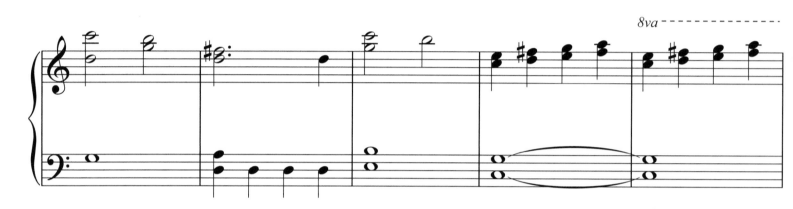

LOVE

By DAVID FOSTER

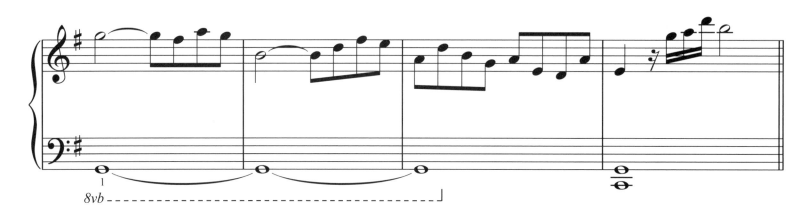

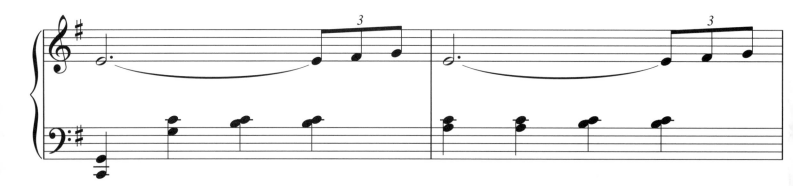

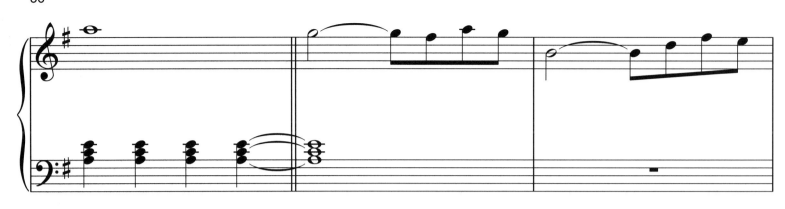

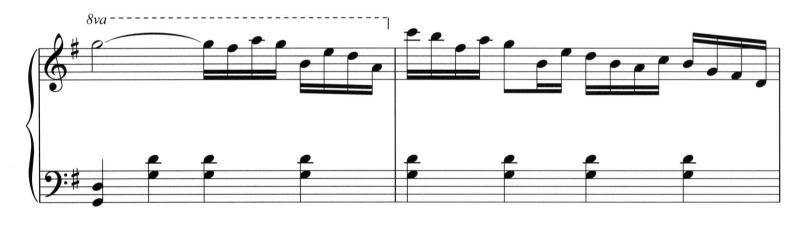

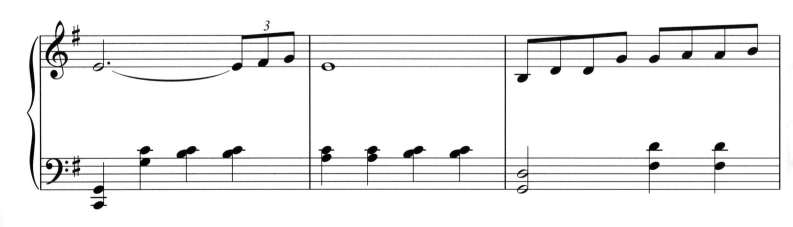

LOVE'S RETURN

By DAVID LANZ

39

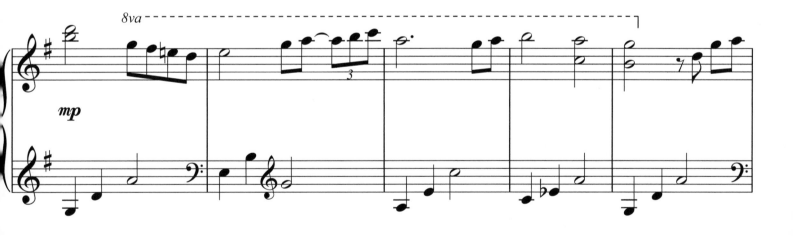

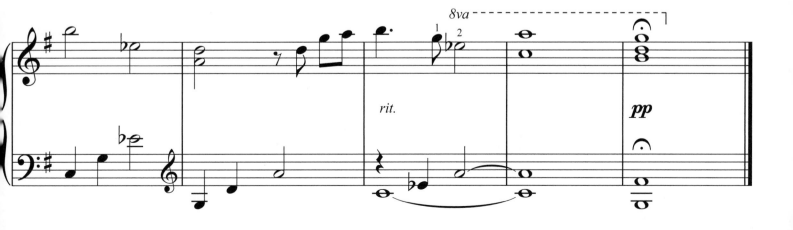

A MOMENT LOST

By DAVID NEVUE

Slowly, expressively

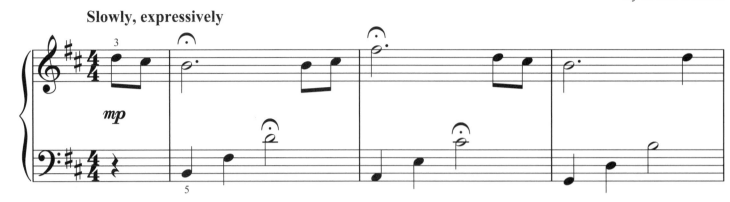

Slightly faster, expressively

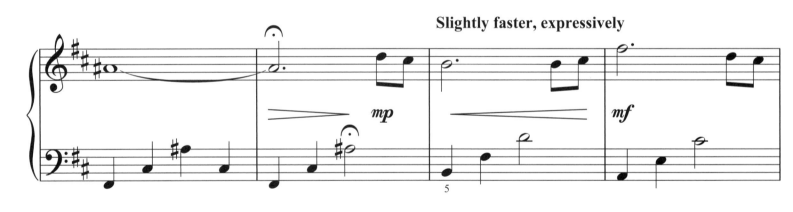

Faster, very freely

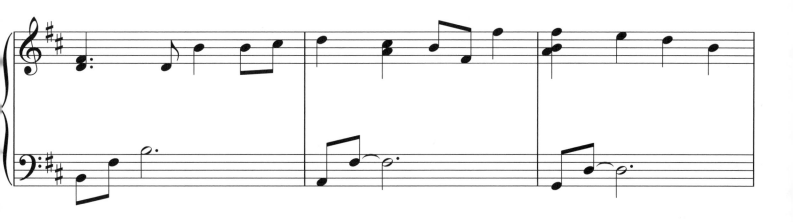

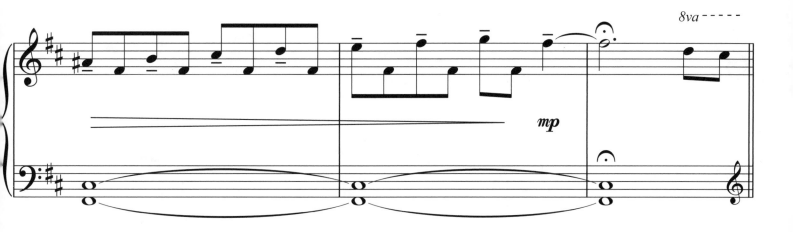

Slowly, expressively

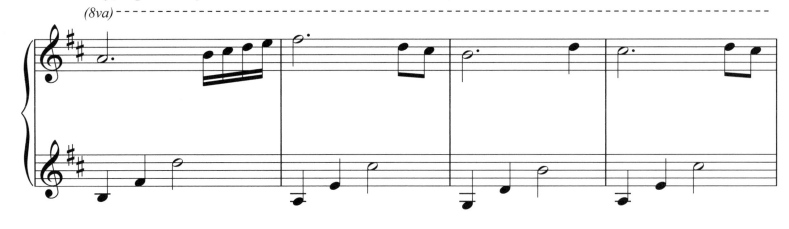

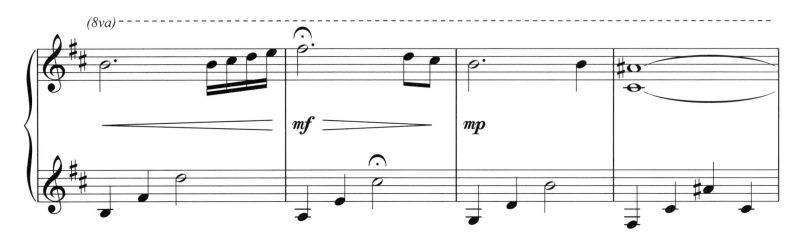

Faster, very freely

Slower, heavily

46

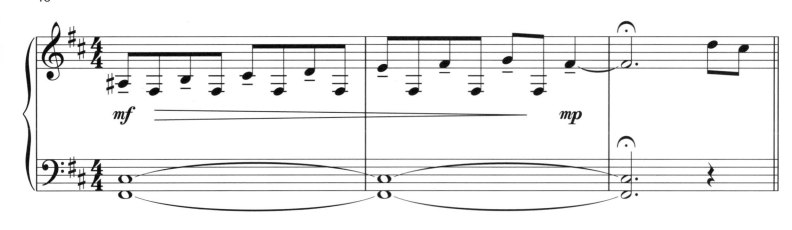

Slowly, expressively

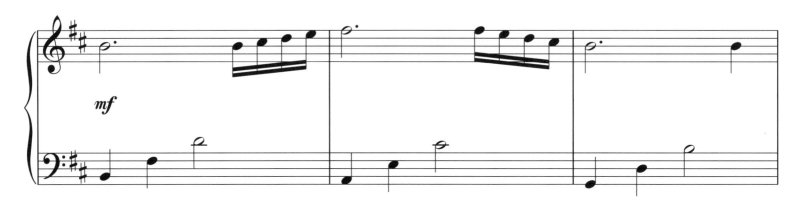

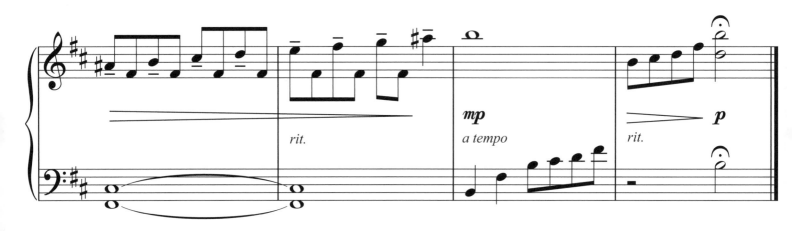

PORZ GORET

By YANN TIERSON

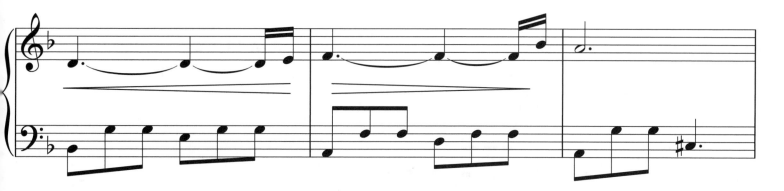

NOCTURNE IN A MINOR

Written by
CHAD LAWSON

Serene, with freedom

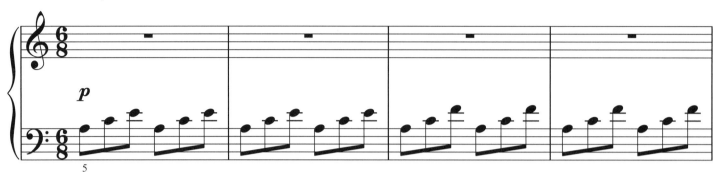

Slightly faster

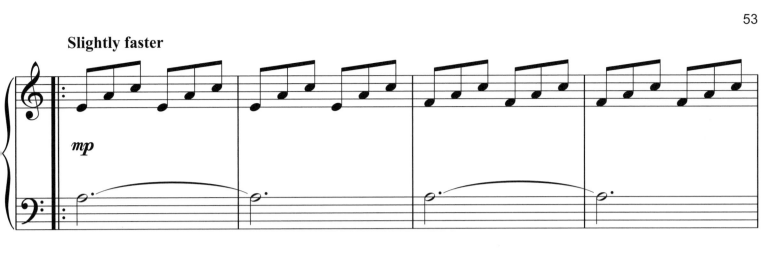

mp

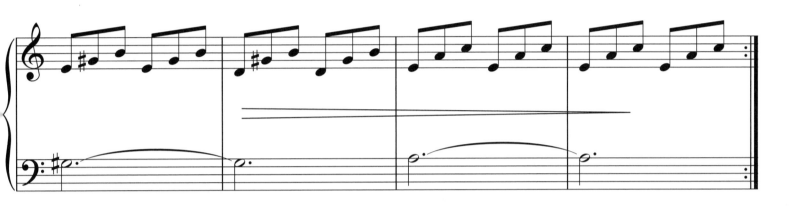

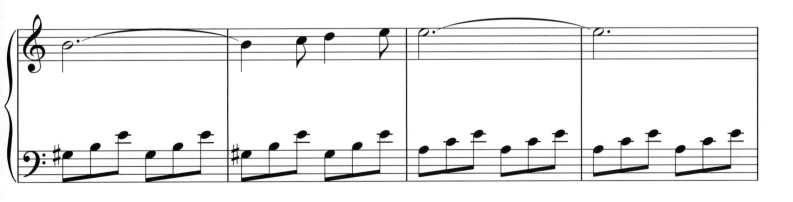

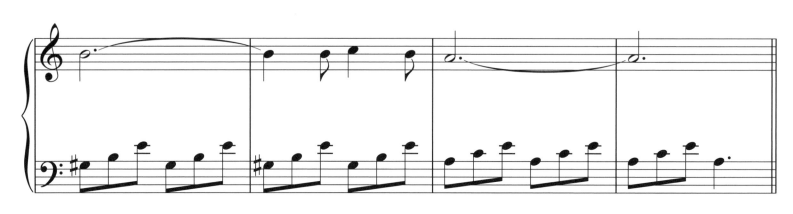

Slower

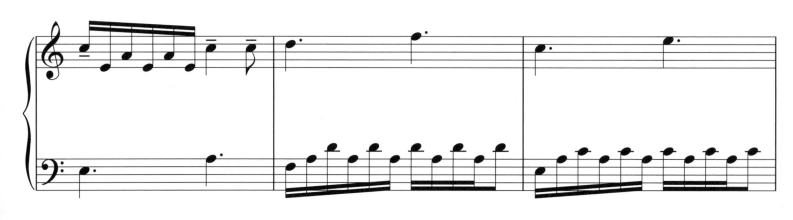

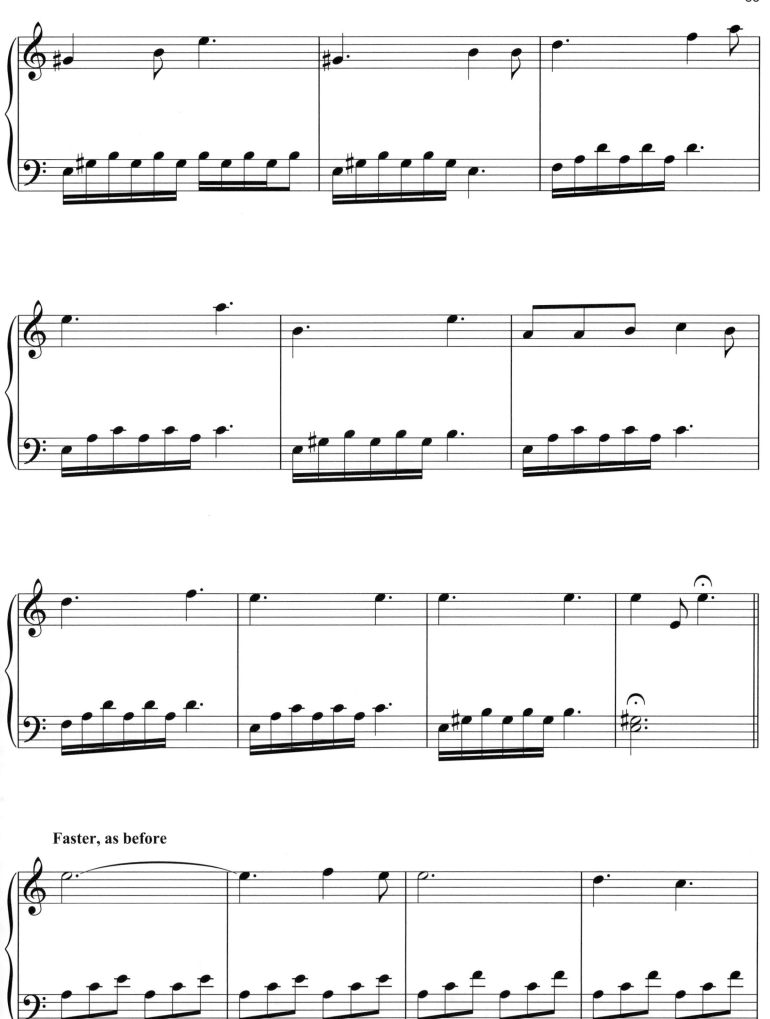

Faster, as before

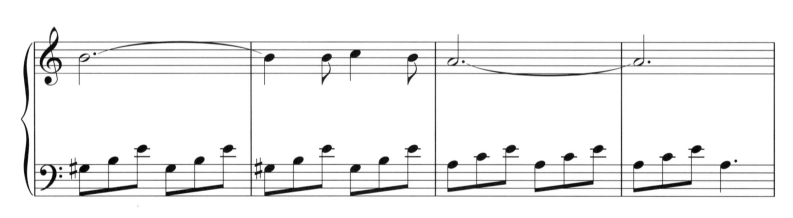

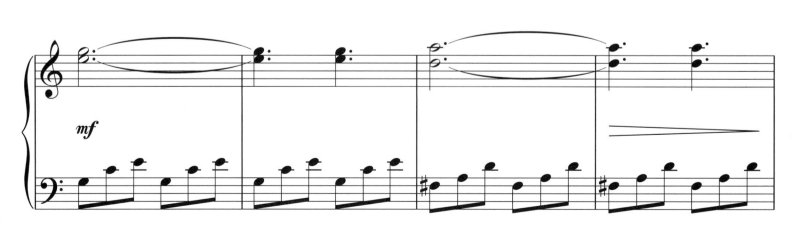

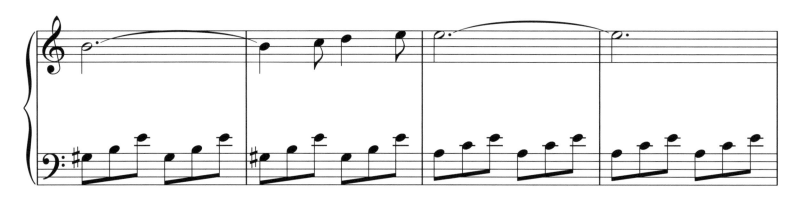

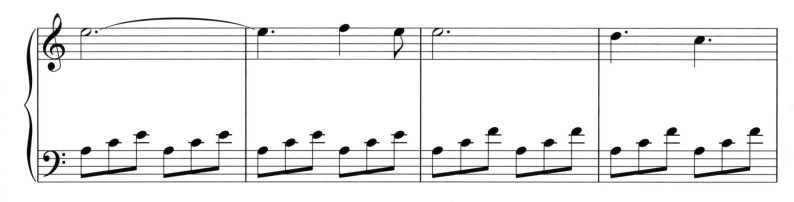

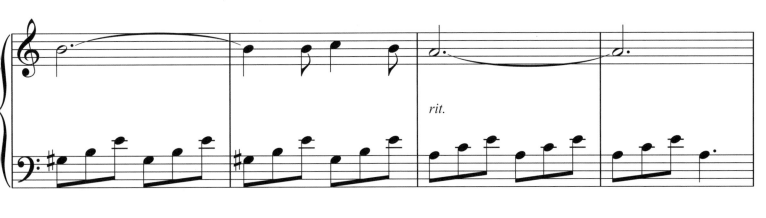

Slower, soaring

ONE SUMMER'S DAY

from SPIRITED AWAY

By JOE HISAISHI

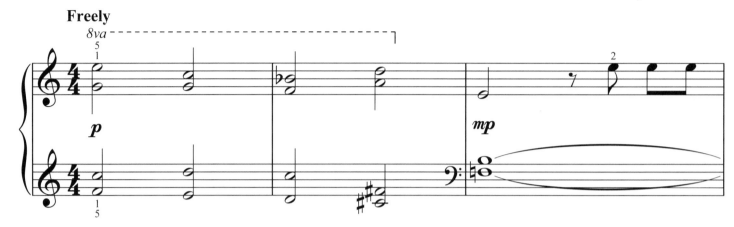

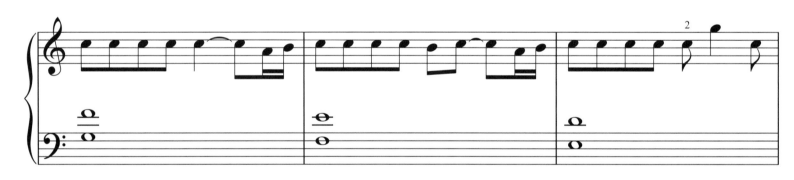

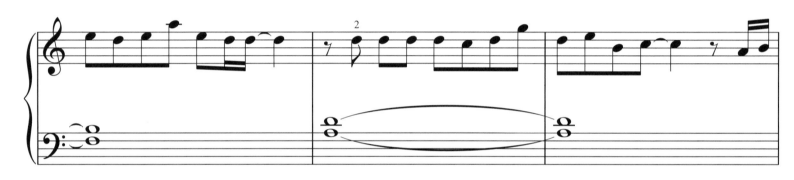

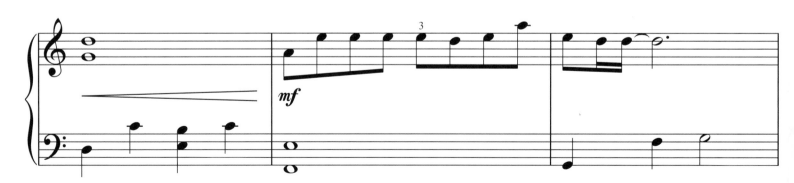

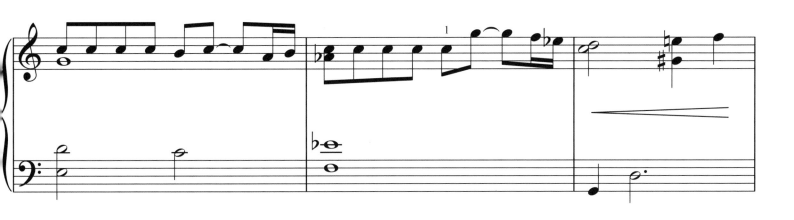

ROMANCES

Music by DAVID LINDGREN ZACHARIAS,
OLOF CARL JOHAN OLSON, EMANUEL OLSSON,
ERIK HOLMBERG and ANDERS PETTERSON

Flowing, with feeling

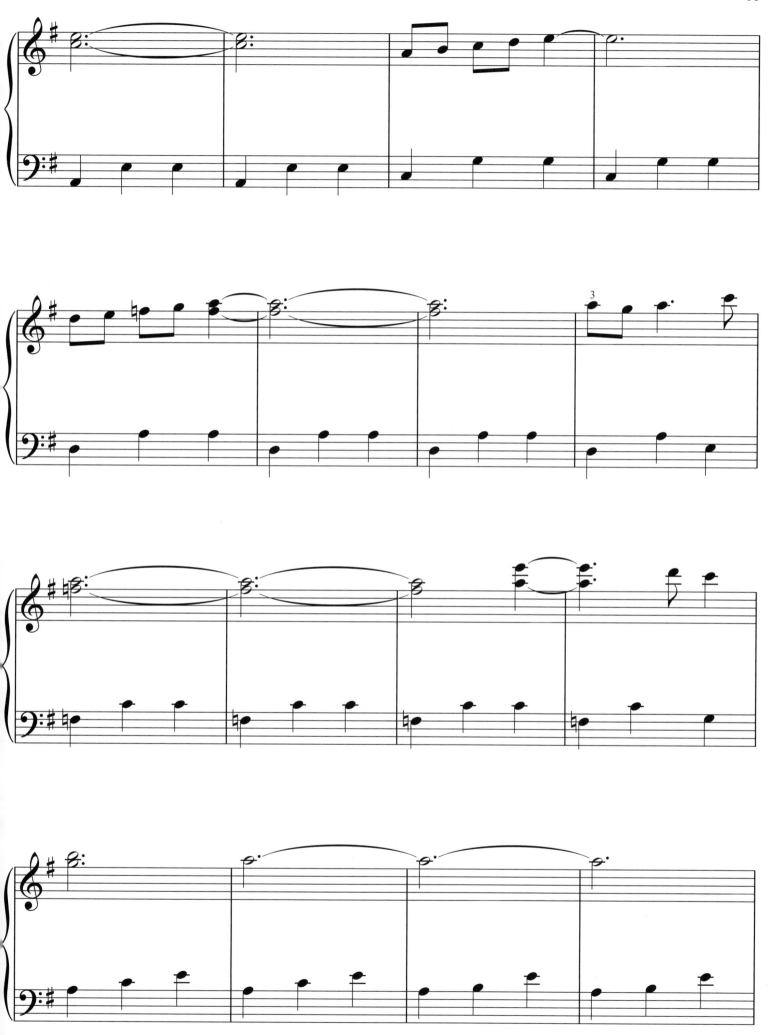

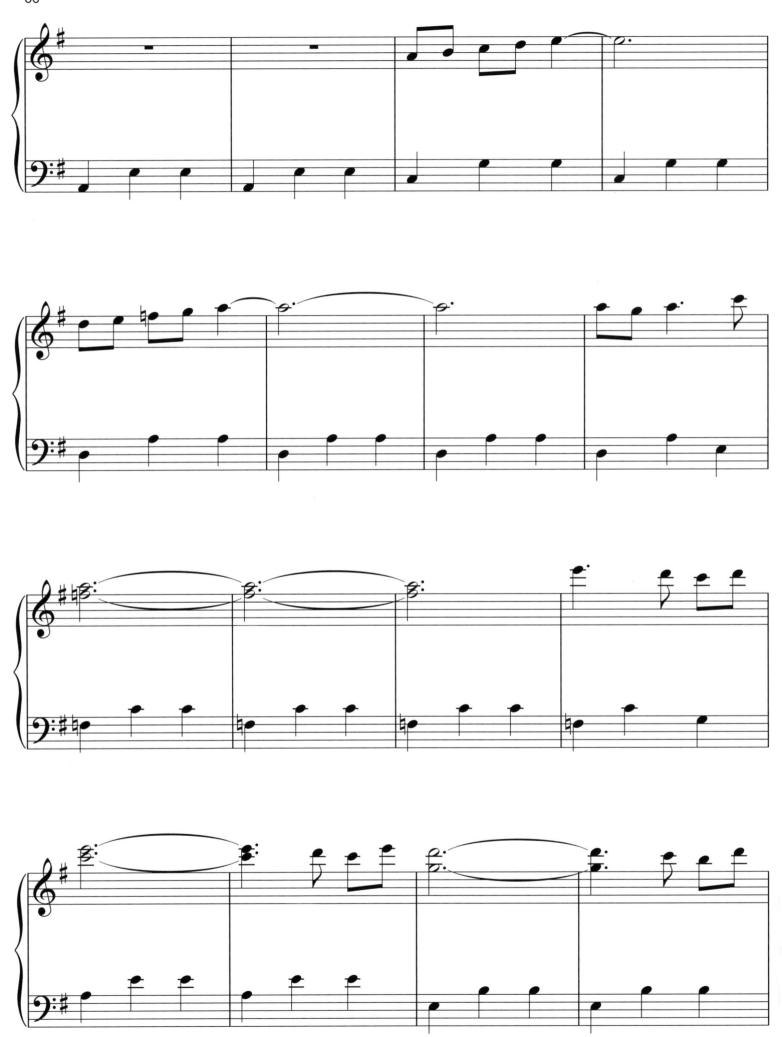

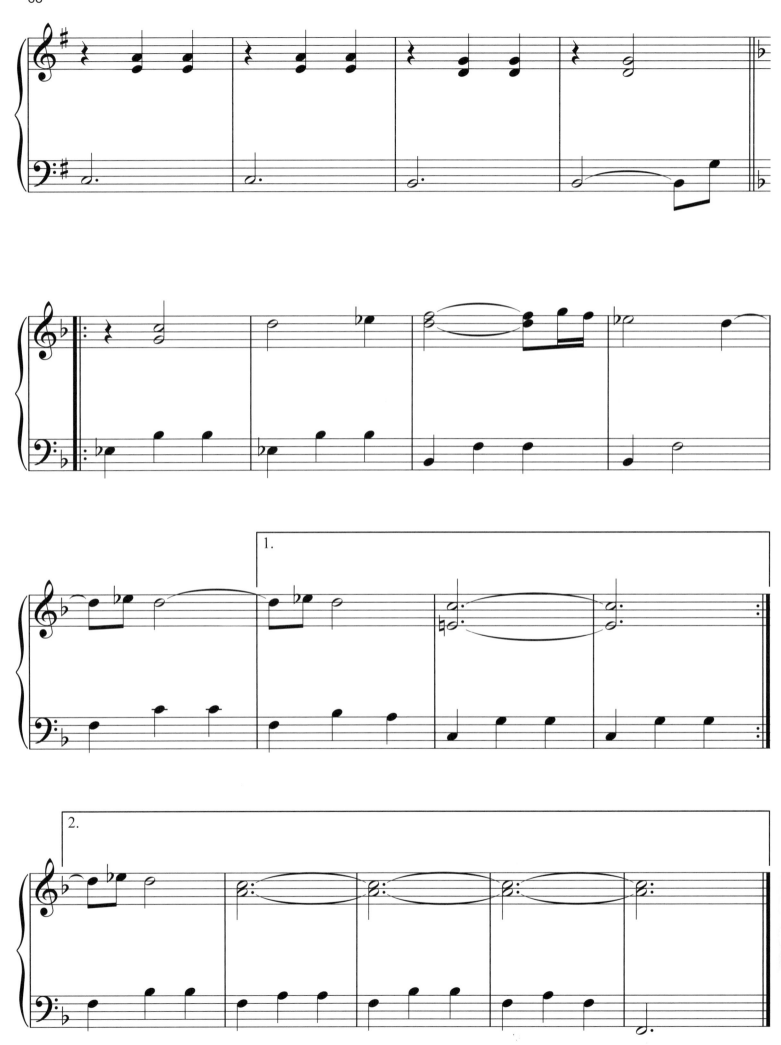

SEPTEMBER SONG

Words and Music by
AGNES OBEL

Flowing, in 2

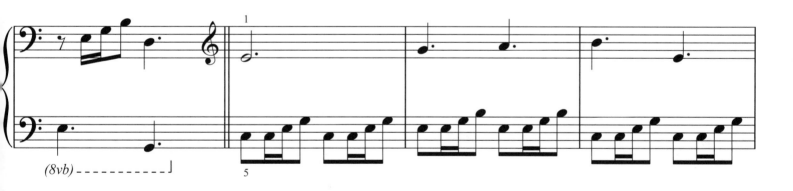

To Coda ⊕

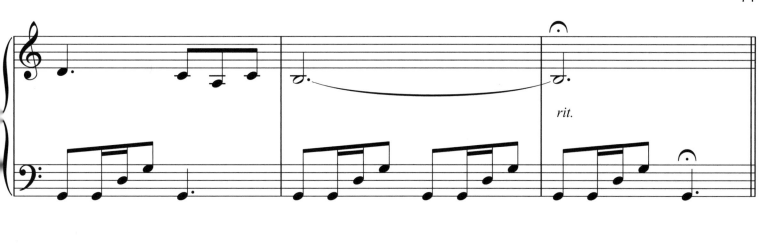

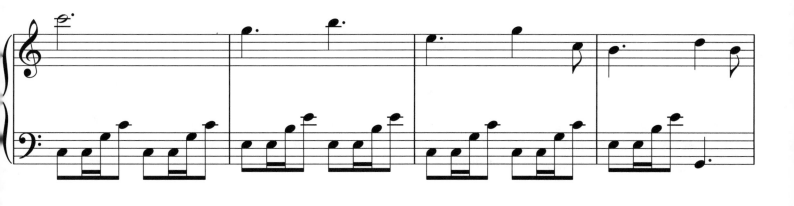

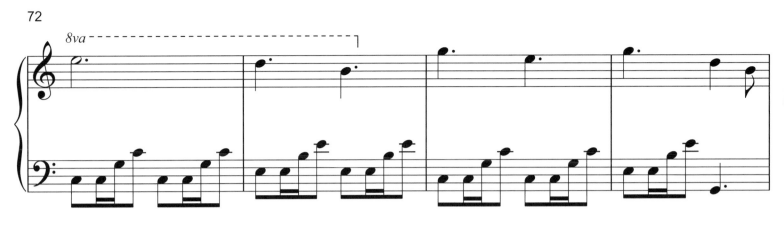

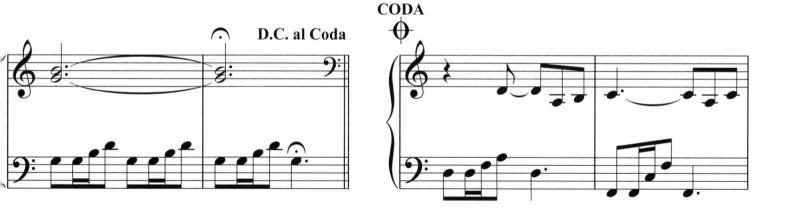

D.C. al Coda

CODA

rit.

SEA CHANGE

By STEPHAN MOCCIO

Poetically and inspired

UNA MATTINA

Music by
LUDOVICO EINAUDI

Lightly

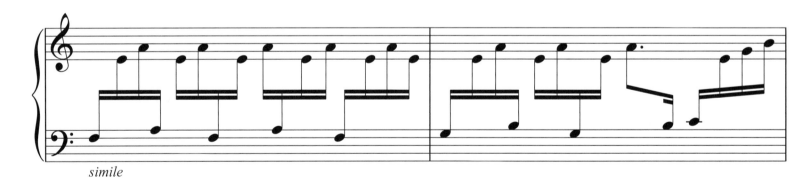

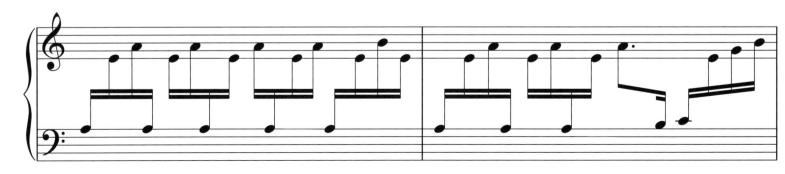

WHEN MORNING COMES

By PAUL CARDALL

Slowly, in 2

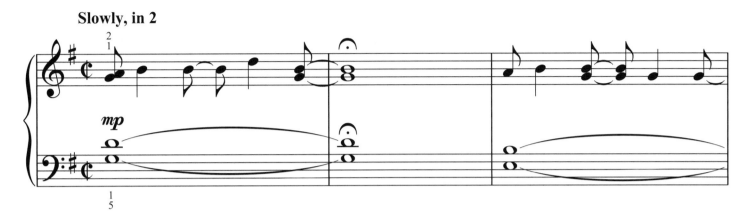

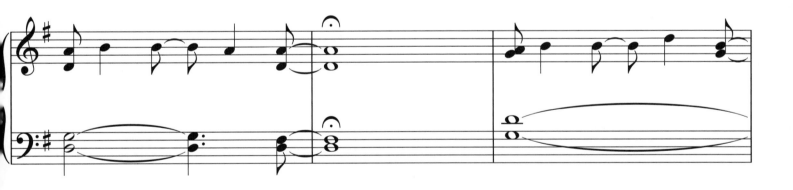

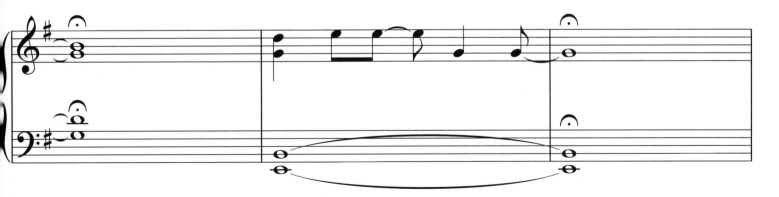

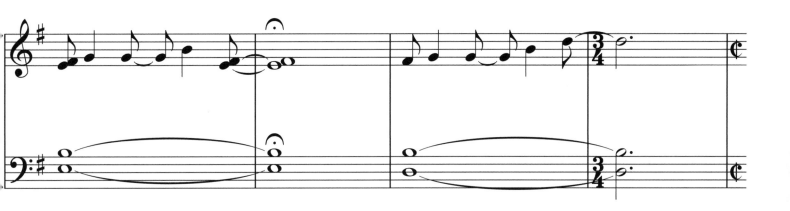

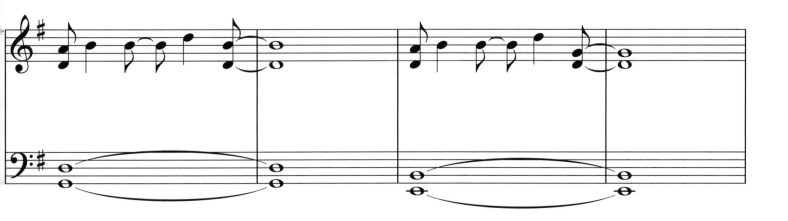

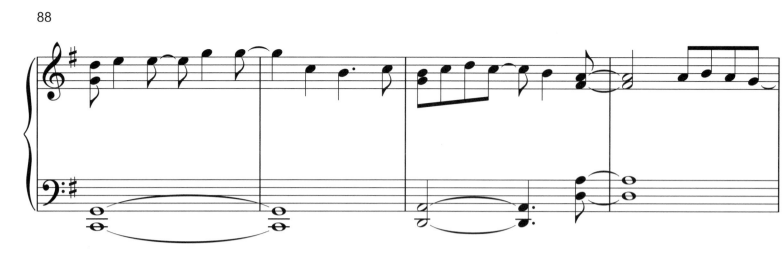

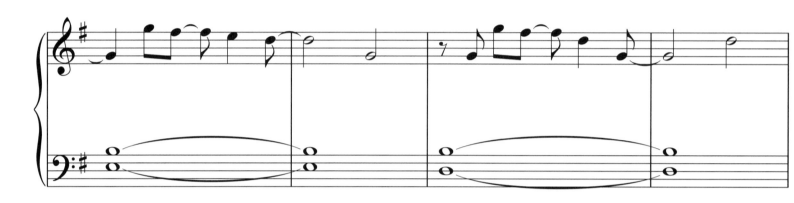

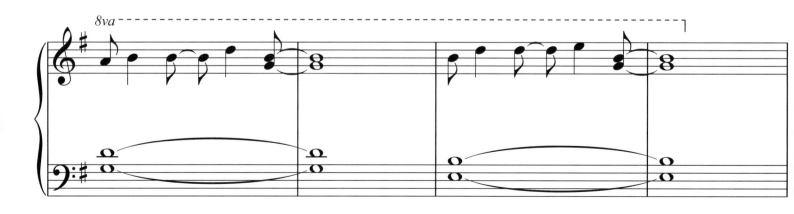

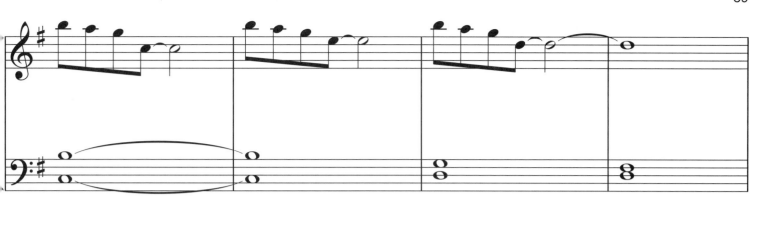

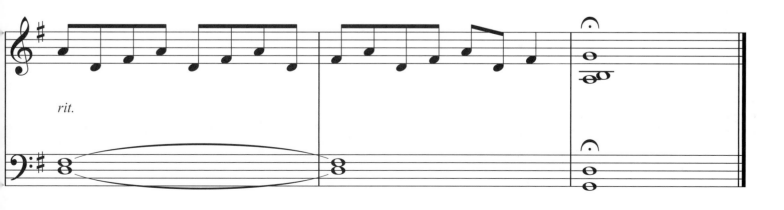

WINGED MELANCHOLY

Music by
PATRICK HAMILTON

Sweet and gentle with some rubato

poco rall.

a tempo

rall.

molto rall.

WRITTEN ON THE SKY

Composed by
MAX RICHTER

Expressively

SUPER EASY SONGBOOK

It's super easy! This series features accessible arrangements for piano, with simple right-hand melody, letter names inside each note, and basic left-hand chord diagrams. Perfect for players of all ages!

THE BEATLES
00198161 60 songs.....................$15.99

BEAUTIFUL BALLADS
00385162 50 songs.....................$14.99

BEETHOVEN
00345533 21 selections.............$9.99

BEST SONGS EVER
00329877 60 songs.....................$15.99

BROADWAY
00193871 60 songs.....................$15.99

JOHNNY CASH
00287524 20 songs.....................$9.99

CHART HITS
00380277 24 songs.....................$12.99

CHRISTMAS CAROLS
00277955 60 songs.....................$15.99

CHRISTMAS SONGS
00236850 60 songs.....................$15.99

CHRISTMAS SONGS WITH 3 CHORDS
00367423 30 songs.....................$10.99

CLASSIC ROCK
00287526 60 songs.....................$15.99

CLASSICAL
00194693 60 selections............$15.99

COUNTRY
00285257 60 songs.....................$15.99

DISNEY
00199558 60 songs.....................$15.99

BOB DYLAN
00364487 22 songs.....................$12.99

BILLIE EILISH
00346515 22 songs.....................$10.99

FOLKSONGS
00381031 60 songs.....................$15.99

FOUR CHORD SONGS
00249533 60 songs.....................$15.99

FROZEN COLLECTION
00334069 14 songs.....................$10.99

GEORGE GERSHWIN
00345536 22 songs.....................$9.99

GOSPEL
00285256 60 songs.....................$15.99

HIT SONGS
00194367 60 songs.....................$15.99

HYMNS
00194659 60 songs.....................$15.99

JAZZ STANDARDS
00233687 60 songs.....................$15.99

BILLY JOEL
00329996 22 songs.....................$10.99

ELTON JOHN
00298762 22 songs.....................$10.99

KIDS' SONGS
00198009 60 songs.....................$15.99

LEAN ON ME
00350593 22 songs.....................$9.99

THE LION KING
00303511 9 songs.....................$9.99

ANDREW LLOYD WEBBER
00249580 48 songs.....................$19.99

MOVIE SONGS
00233670 60 songs.....................$15.99

PEACEFUL MELODIES
00367880 60 songs.....................$16.99

POP SONGS FOR KIDS
00346809 60 songs.....................$16.99

POP STANDARDS
00233770 60 songs.....................$15.99

QUEEN
00294889 20 songs.....................$10.99

ED SHEERAN
00287525 20 songs.....................$9.99

SIMPLE SONGS
00329906 60 songs.....................$15.99

STAR WARS (EPISODES I-IX)
00345560 17 songs.....................$10.99

TAYLOR SWIFT
00323195 22 songs.....................$10.99

THREE CHORD SONGS
00249664 60 songs.....................$15.99

TOP HITS
00300405 22 songs.....................$10.99

WORSHIP
00294871 60 songs.....................$15.99

HAL•LEONARD®
www.halleonard.com

Disney characters and artwork TM & © 2021 Disney

Prices, contents and availability subject to change without notice.